Why am I Involved with a Jerk

...

AGAIN?

By

Charles K. Summers

https://charlesksummers.com

Why am I Involved with a Jerk ... AGAIN?
by Charles K. Summers

Library of Congress Control Number: 2025911489

Paperback: ISBN-13: 978-0-615-84587-6
e-book: ISBN-13: 978-1-7349129-7-5

Washington – USA

Self-help Techniques

Dedication

For Eleanor Rigby, Nowhere Men and Women, and all who search for, and deserve, loving supportive relationships

&

For my beloved wife Marie, and friends Mariló Costa and Janet Coffin for plowing through this manuscript.

Table of Contents

Prologue

This book has been simmering for almost 45 years. Although I felt that it would be a useful book, I didn't think there was a chance in the world to find a publisher. I hold no seminars. I give no lectures. I don't have a television show, a webcast, or a podcast (I do have a blog and a Substack newsletter). I am not a celebrity in any way. What I do have is experience and a personality that observes and analyzes.

The genesis of this book arose from two sources. The first was my experience as a moderator, in the 1980s, for an online discussions forum dealing with human sexuality and dating. As a moderator, one of my duties was to initiate discussion threads. For one such, I asked people about what qualities to which they were attracted. It became a lively thread with many responses. However, when I pointed out that what they were listing were relationship "wish lists" and that, based on previous discussions, these were not the qualities to which they were attracted, the thread became an inferno.

Obviously, this was a difficult, and highly emotional, subject for the people in the forum. These were people who had talked at great length about the "jerks" with whom they had been involved – all the qualities that made them feel that it was not a good relationship for them. Yet, the next relationship (I was part of the forum for almost five years) didn't get any better. One obvious thing was in common with all of their failed relationships – they chose the people. They **chose** to be involved with these "jerks". Why? These people did **not** satisfy the qualities desired (as stated on "wish lists") but were still chosen. It was apparent that there was a hidden list of attributes to which they were attracted – an "attraction list". For these repeat failed relationships, the "wish list" and the "attraction list" did not match.

The second impetus for this book was an article from *Ms.* Magazine to which I had been a subscriber for many years. This was a front cover article about six women in abusive relationships. The article focused on the qualities that made the relationships abusive. I believe that the intent was to show women how to recognize that they were in an abusive relationship. While this was, and is, a worthy objective, I felt that something else would have been more useful. These women were strong, intelligent, successful, talented, and attractive – able to pick between many different men (at that time, only heterosexual relationships were considered). Yet they chose these men. Why?

I might as well say this in the prologue. This book isn't aimed at specifically YOU. Each one of us is a unique, special, person in this universe. There is no way that this book can be directed towards you. Generalizations will be made. Stereotypes will be used. One thing may bring self-recognition and something else will say "hey, that's not me". If one personality type in a scenario doesn't fit, try the other role. Perhaps your gender role does not fit neatly into a "he"/"she" pair. Perhaps the relationship is between two (or more) individuals of the same (or similar) gender. Hopefully, this set of notes can still be of use. Use what seems to apply, change pronouns, and proceed with what is going to your own unique partnership.

If you truly want to have something aimed specifically at you then find a matchmaker with 20 years of experience, a PhD in personality development or relationship interactions, AND in a well-functioning long-term relationship.

A single relationship doesn't really indicate anything. We can all be "fooled". Perhaps we can also be fooled in different ways at different times. However, as the saying goes: "Fool me once, shame on you. Fool me twice, shame on me". This book is for those people who find themselves involved with a jerk ... AGAIN.

Chapter 1: What is a Jerk?

Everyone knows what a jerk is, don't they? Apple's internal dictionary says it is a "contemptibly obnoxious person". Alas, this really only delays the definition to another level. What is "contemptible"? What is "obnoxious"? We could look up those words also but, at root, it ends up being a description of someone with whom you don't enjoy interacting.

Anyone Can be a Jerk.

A jerk can be anyone. It does not apply to a specific gender, eye coloration, religious or ethnic background, physical size, body type, social or monetary class, pigmentation, or age. However, it is certainly possible for a jerk of a category to establish, or reinforce, stereotypes about that category. People often focus on attributes that are relatively easy to define and then connect them to behaviors. If a woman is involved with a male jerk then

1

they will be more wary about males in general – anticipating other men to have the same, or similar, "jerky" behaviors. Of course, the reality is that he was a jerk who happened to be a man – not that all men are jerks.

Jerks are also not associated with a particular place or environment. Should we ever encounter sapient people on another planet, I would expect a good chance for there to be jerks there. There can be jerks in the office and jerks at a restaurant. Since being a jerk is associated with one or more unappreciated personality points, the only way a group of people can be guaranteed to not have any jerks would be if they were a "group mind". For example, if we encountered an alien race organized like a colony of bees then they would either ALL be jerks or none of them.

No "Universal" Jerks.

Just as anyone can be a jerk, it is also true that it is unlikely for a person to be considered a jerk by everyone else. Even Adolph Hitler was apparently loved by Eva Braun and had a number of supporters who continued to support him after the revelations of atrocities authorized and committed. One can say, of course, that he was part of a community of jerks. During political election campaigns, and during legislative battles, one side often feels the other is a jerk (or group of jerks) while the other side feels equally confident that they are great and the first group consists of jerks.

Within the context of dating, what this basically means is that your jerk may be someone else's angel. So -- let them be with that someone else. This book is about the jerk in **your** life and how you can stop being repeatedly involved with jerks. It is not your responsibility (or even healthy) to try to change yourself such that the other person no longer seems like a jerk. Nor can you change anyone other than yourself. While change is always possible, change must be self-motivated. The person has to **want** to change. There is certainly no motivation for the person to change while you patiently await spontaneous metamorphosis.

This statement will be occasionally repeated, in one form or another, throughout this book – "You cannot change others. Others only change when they are self-motivated to do so."

Transitional versus Permanent Jerks.

It is possible that a person will not always be a jerk. If they are, then they are a "permanent jerk" (note that, as always, this means a jerk in your particular eyes). They may also be a jerk only from time to time – a "transitional jerk". If you ever find yourself saying "don't be a jerk" to someone then they are probably only a transitional jerk. There are different types of transitional jerks. One type is only a jerk in certain environments. Another is a jerk during certain situations. It is possible to be a jerk towards a subset of people based on irrelevant criteria. There are certainly other scenarios where a person can be a jerk only during that scenario. The main point is that, for the rest of the time, they are not jerks.

Does this mean that you **DO** want to remain with that person? That's a subjective choice and not an easy one and certainly a choice that only you can make. But make it a conscious choice and not just something that you do because it is easier to continue along. I don't like changing dentists, or banks, or insurance agents because the upfront challenges of change make it unappealing. That doesn't mean that, in the long run, a change isn't for the best – and most people's objectives in relationships are for the long run. (For people who do have only short-term objectives in relationships, constant change is part of the game.)

Why are certain people jerks in particular scenarios? A lot of the time, there is something uncomfortable for them in that place, situation, environment, or with that other group of people. This discomfort causes them to short-circuit their normal self-monitoring – to jump ahead and act or speak before thinking. Most two-year-olds are highly egocentric and, if they weren't so awfully cute, might be considered jerks. This phase is referred to as the "terrible twos". People usually grow out of that – they learn to socialize appropriately with others especially within their peer group and accustomed environment. Transitional jerks can find themselves regressed back to early childhood behaviors.

The point of this book, and the likely focus for your interest in this book, is not to figure out precisely why a person is sometimes a jerk. Rather, it is to decide if the person is the "right" one for you to be with within a relationship. I will assume that you, yourself, are not certain about this or you wouldn't be reading this. Overall, the main point is that sometimes people are jerks only at certain times and it is up to you to decide whether the other times make it worthwhile to tolerate the bad times. Toleration is an important, and necessary, part of relationships but make it a conscious choice.

"Googly-eyed Stage".

The point at which people often say "I didn't know he/she was a jerk" is after they have been with the person a while. The initial stage, before this reanalysis period, is known by various terms – the honeymoon phase, the infatuation phase, the courtship phase, and so forth. I prefer to call it the "googly-eyed stage". There is an inherent biological aspect of this initial meeting and involvement that physically blocks out some of the "higher brain" functions and actually prevents analysis. This is all part of the circle of life trying to perpetuate the species.

In other words, give yourself a break if you find that you've ignored some important personality traits at the beginning of a relationship. However, once again, the assumption is that you are interested in having a happy, healthy, long-term relationship. Thus, even at this stage, you will improve your chances if you can more clearly evaluate the other person.

Time.

A relationship does have different stages – and it has slightly different stages depending on whether it evolves slowly over a period of years while each person is still developing or whether it is part of a deliberate courtship/dating situation. A "childhood romance" exists when two people grow up together, then start dating, then finally form a relationship. This can sometimes work very well – IF the individuals involved have been open to examining others such that it is truly a choice.

Most relationships start with the dating/courtship phase. As mentioned above, the first stage (after initially "giving it a try") may have some initial blindness towards the other's personality traits which will eventually disappear. Try to clear the veils as quickly as possible – you aren't actually doing the other person a favor to ignore things that may eventually cause even greater pain at a postponed, but necessary, breakup. The next few sections will go into some methods that may help to evaluate even during the initial period.

How do They Behave Towards Those with Less Power?

There is a maxim about evaluating leaders. This is a matter of seeing how they behave towards those who have less power. If they are a corporate officer, see how they behave towards the janitorial staff. If they are a shopper, see how they behave towards the cashier, sales people, and other store personnel. It is only within the context of not having fears of repercussions that their personality aspects towards other people can fairly be evaluated. In other contexts, they may be a self-restrained jerk but they're still a jerk and it is likely you will be the target of that behavior at some point in time.

How do they talk about people who are not around? If they say things about people that they would not be willing to say to their face, this says something about them to which you should listen carefully. The main point is that, especially during the early stage of a relationship, it may be easier to evaluate their personality based on how they treat other people rather than how you perceive they are treating you.

Animals.

In many ways, the treatment of animals is another perspective on how they behave towards those with less power. This does not require them to be a vegetarian – it is the treatment of living animals that is relevant. There are also many reasons why they may have problems interacting with animals including allergies, phobias, and life incidents. These are attributes to note because it may affect the relationship but they are not, in themselves, an indication of personality traits that may cause them to achieve jerkdom.

How do they actively interact with animals? I won't say there is a "correct" way to do this although if the person dissects live animals then I, personally, would say that is fairly direct evidence of a personality that **I** would prefer to avoid. See if you like the way that they interact with animals – if so, that is a good sign.

Humor.

We are moving away from jerkdom a bit here but, in terms of compatibility, humor is very important. If she laughs at something until she is rolling on the floor and you, experiencing the same event, are ready to throw up then do you really want to spend a lot of time with her? When he laughs, are you looking around the room searching for a donkey? While the manner in which a person laughs does not mean they are a jerk, it is also very unlikely that they will change the way they laugh. If you do not like the way they laugh, expect to have to tolerate it for the length of the relationship.

Subjective.

One thing should be apparent from this chapter – the quality of being a jerk is completely subjective. To repeat, one person's jerk may be another person's angel. It is possible that someone that you consider to be a jerk will also be considered a jerk by many other people. You may be the only one who feels that they are a jerk. It is the way you feel that is the most important criterion.

Chapter 2: Your Wish List

Matchmaker, make a match for me. When we look for someone to be with us in a relationship, we have things that we want. This is commonly referred to as a "wish list". A wish list can be for friendship, romance, family, or whatever is needed from a relationship. Wish lists also exist for other things – a new car, a vacation, or something else of which we have choices to make. When a person recognizes that physical life won't continue forever, the wish list becomes a "bucket list". This chapter will concentrate on the relationship wish list.

Explicit versus Implicit Wish Lists.

"Everyone" knows what a wish list is, right? It is that list of attributes that "Mr./Miss/Ms. Right" must have before you want to be involved with them. However, when I did some Internet searching for relationship, or dating, wish lists, I found that they were few and far between. Perhaps it isn't something that people like to share on the public Internet?

At any rate, the wish lists that I have seen break things down into three categories. These categories can be labeled physical, social (including economic), and personal. Yes, these can be broken down into different names and different splits. Physical can be broken into "attractiveness", "hygiene", "healthiness", number of legs, and so forth. Social can include career, how much money they make, number of clubs to which they belong, and so forth. Personal is just another way of saying that they have likes and dislikes and, thus, the list is a reflection of your own likes and dislikes. Keep that broccoli away from me! Extra anchovies on that pizza please! Any color but blue, if you don't mind!

An example of a wish list (for someone seeking a male) might be as follows:

5' 10" or taller
Weight proportionate to height
Keeps his hair and body clean
Loyal and faithful
Is positive about life
Can talk about various topics – not just sports
Takes pride in his work – wants to do his best
Wants a family but has no children yet
Loves southern cooking

Responsible
Enjoys hiking and walks in the park

All of these sound pretty reasonable, don't they? And they are. Wish lists are good ways to note the things that you hope for in the future and how someone else might be able to be a positive part of that future. The above list is probably shorter than an average-sized list but it is better to keep the list short – or to prioritize the list. It is also a good idea to keep the list positive – what you DO want rather than what you do NOT want.

Some people keep a physical, written, list to which they can refer from time to time. Others just keep the list internally – in their minds, waiting for circumstances in which they may decide to change it or review it. Probably everyone keeps some type of internal list although, stereotypically, for men it may limit itself to physical attributes.

Physical and Internal.

Your wish list may very well contain physical aspects of the person. As much as I would like to say that such is not important, the reality is that it can make a large difference

AT THE BEGINNING of a relationship. It may cause you to downgrade other criteria, it may cause "chemistry", it may rev up various hormonal responses.

Physical qualities should not be held against a person – a person who is considered by most to be very attractive may also be an interesting, smart, caring person. Or they may not be. If you find yourself falling prey to physical values overwhelming all other criteria then please help yourself to not make long-term commitments or investments before you get out of the "googly-eyed stage".

As opposed to physical aspects, there are internal aspects. If you examine your wish list carefully, you are very likely to find that internal aspects on the list are not only higher in priority but also more numerous. But you may find physical aspects hard to ignore. Try to wait out the infatuation.

What Happens with your Wish List.

So, you have a wish list – whether it is internal or external. How do you make use of it? It is very unlikely that you bring it out every time you meet people. Do you get near someone and start examining that person based on your wish list? Probably not.

It's probably a good thing that you don't start examining a new acquaintance based on your wish list. In the first place, there are many different reasons to meet people and not just based on desires within a romantic relationship. Your best friend may be waiting to be found around the corner. A long-term connection that will help you with your career may be connected to the next hand that you shake. Or, perhaps, the person you meet will know other people who will be people that you will value having in your life.

You meet someone and you feel the sparks fly. There is a good chance that, within the space of a few minutes, you have placed the person into a category. That category may be potential friend, new romance, business acquaintance, or interesting person. There is also a good chance that, within that same few minutes, you have placed that person into an unfavorable category – a "loser", unattractive, "no chemistry", boring, or even a "jerk".

Now it comes to the possible use of your wish list – when you get home or when you are by yourself for a while. You start imagining the qualities of the people you have met based on your wish list – but only those people that you have already placed in the potential new romance category. Note that you have already eliminated most of the possible candidates – some of them "forever" – before you ever examine them through the lens of your wish list. This may be a mistake. When you are reviewing people, open your net and put others through your criteria even if you initially feel "maybe not".

If You are Following your Wish List, Why is He/She/They a Jerk?

As described above, your wish list is not likely to be the first criteria that you use upon meeting people. Perhaps you looked it over, or reviewed it, before going to the place where you met new people. If so, then you may have had one or two of the criteria from that list in mind. However, you have now made the first level of choice as to whether you want to attempt to give more time to certain people. If one of the people strongly appealed to you on a potentially romantic level, you may already be at the first step of the "googly-eyed stage".

"Following" your Wish List.

The chances are excellent that, when you review your "candidates" according to your wish list, you will find that it is hard to reconcile them with your wish list. As mentioned earlier, usually you do not split apart the wish list from the attraction list until later in the relationship. But the more that you understand the distinction, and the better able you are in examining the people you meet based on your wish list, the sooner you can start to understand why you have elevated them into a better position. This is not the point in time to decide to discard any possibilities. They may be that special person – never say never.

Chapter 3: History and the Attraction List

The people in the online group that I mediated got really mad when I pointed out that their "wish lists" did not seem to match well against the characteristics that they described existed in recent relationships. People like to think they are in control – in control of themselves and in control of decisions and reactions. We can be, but it's on a sliding scale based on patience with oneself and self-awareness. I doubt very much that any human is ALWAYS in conscious control of their decisions and reactions.

What is an Attraction List?

So, if these "attraction lists" do not correspond directly with our "wish lists", where do they come from? Without getting too deep into psychobabble, it is part of your subconscious. You can split it up into id, ego, and superego, if you want. There is a part of you that may surface in dreams and has an influence, without conscious awareness or thought, in almost everything you do.

I grew up in a matriarchal family with a misandrist mother who wanted a daughter (and couldn't, due to complications leading to a hysterectomy). Since she had two sons (and only two sons), you can guess that this caused a lot of problems. Besides going through five husbands/marriages, her feelings were an integral part of her actions, reactions, and decisions. After 14 years of therapy, I finally reached the point where I was content to be a male. Not very close to a stereotypical male – but content to be a male.

Did she do anything explicitly that said "don't trust men, don't be a man"? No. But it was part of the environment. My brother and I reacted differently and approached life and our development differently but it definitely affected both of us.

Your "attraction list" will be shaped by your history and your past interactions with other people. A lot of it will be based on early childhood environments. This isn't necessarily a direct reflection. "Marry a woman just like mom." "My daddy wouldn't have done it that way, I shouldn't do it that way." Much is associated with a feeling that "this is what a home is like. This is what a relationship is like."

An Attraction List is NOT your Wish List.

Such as with me, therapy and counseling can bring awareness to you of factors within your subconscious. That does not mean it eliminates it. I was attracted to specific qualities, partially based on how I was treated, and my father was treated, growing up. I am STILL attracted to those qualities but I have some conscious awareness and that allows me to buffer reactions and make more-or-less sane, and deliberate, decisions rather than being a puppet of my subconscious. It also means I have a built-in "radar" and have very good reliability at being able to detect, and identify, those characteristics to which I am attracted. (This has, in the past, led me to telling others about problems that I have perceived. Correct or not, it was not appropriate for me to discuss such.)

A child growing up in an abusive household will consider that to be a normal environment. (It is also true that a child growing up in a loving, caring household will consider THAT to be a normal environment.) After leaving the nest, one may lean many directions. I am not qualified to state the whens and whys but you may become an abusive person or you may become a person who seeks abuse. Once aware of the inappropriateness of your childhood, you may become an advocate for people who have been abused in the same way. However, that environment will make a difference to your attraction list.

Moving past morbid and dysfunctional backgrounds, we are still influenced by childhood, family, and interactions with others as we have grown up. As is true with less desirable experiences, a person can react different ways. If your mother had red hair – and you had a positive relationship with her – you may find yourself attracted to red hair. (If you did NOT get along with your mother, you may either be attracted to or move away from women with red hair.)

Static qualities, such as hair color, are easy to track down and be listed in your wish list. These are usually also in your attraction list. Behaviors are different because few of us take specific note of behaviors or where and when we first encountered them. And, unlike qualities, they are not necessarily obvious. Dad always started the coffee and took a cup in to mother. Doesn't everybody live like that? Mom didn't mind washing dishes but always wanted someone else to dry? Isn't that always true? Mom and dad showered together and then sang together in the restroom after brushing their teeth? So, what's the big deal about that?

How do We Bring the Contents of a Wish List to our Conscious Mind?

So, if an "attraction list" is primarily based on items, and behaviors, that we are not consciously aware of, how do we determine the contents of such a list?

The best method is looking at the past. This is even better when able to discuss with a friend who was present along with any person that you were in a relationship with. As was true of the people in the online discussion group, you were attracted to what you got involved with. They may have, or may not have, matched some (or even all) of your wish list – but they were whom you chose to become involved with.

You can certainly concentrate on the behaviors that you hated or were harmful to you. After all, will it really hurt for you to not be consciously aware of positive things that you are attracted to? You want to determine what characteristics, especially negative (according to your evaluation) ones, exist in that "jerk" with whom you were involved.

Once those characteristics are determined, you need to understand how they manifested. How will you be able to detect them in the future. What "obvious" (apparently not obvious to you) signs were present. No fair for the friend to say "shoot, I always knew that was the case". YOU need to be able to get better at noticing the characteristics before involvement. Yes, perhaps you were still in that early, infatuated, state. Your goal is – next time – to do better.

Again, that unwritten and unrecognized "attraction list" will be composed of both static qualities and dynamic behaviors. Determining what they are will help a lot in giving you a chance to be aware of them and mediate your future reactions to them.

Examine the Past, Eliminate the Most Recent.

When you are working with your past, attempting to distinguish the characteristics of the people with whom you were involved, it helps to make use of time distancing. In some ways, time works against you in that you may forget details. But, overall, it helps because most things can be examined dispassionately and those that ignite renewed emotions act as warning flares in that these are characteristics that need to be examined.

You would have to be some type of superhuman to be able to examine your most recent relationship without strong, blinding, emotions. I recommend keeping the time distancing if possible.

Work with a Friend.

Whether you are working with your very first (romantic) relationship or your most recent one, it helps if someone else can provide insight and some distancing. They have a different point-of-view. Not necessarily a BETTER point-of-view but different. One has to note that your friend is also looking at the relationship through the lens of their childhood, relationship histories, and general history.

So, similar to triangulation where one can use multiple signals and directions to pinpoint an accurate location, multiple points-of-view can allow one to better approximate behaviors of people with whom we have gotten involved.

Life History and your Attraction List.

We have already mentioned some of this but your life helps to mold you. There may be a certain aspect of genetic attraction that leads you to remain within your genome grouping but (I believe) MOST of your attraction list will be built up from your environment and what feels "normal" to you.

Physical aspects are the most obvious – with the recognition that sometimes the "obvious" is the most easily overlooked. Tall, short, thin, stocky, hair color, dimples, laughs, tears, and so forth. Note that it can either be something that attracts you or something that will make you want to avoid – depending on the emotional context within which you remember them.

How easily someone laughs (as opposed to the laugh itself), what do they laugh at, how easily do they cry and, once again, what elicits tears? These internal actions which are reflected in the outside are of moderate difficulty in pinpointing.

True interior feelings and behaviors are the most difficult to discern. You may have considerable insight about such in others (perhaps in yourself also, if you are fortunate) – but bringing it out into the open may be too much for you, or even you with several friends, to isolate.

You can only do your best.

Finding a Match or Finding an Opposite.

It would be so much easier if it was always a quid pro quo. My mother had red hair, therefore I am attracted to red hair. Maybe you were shocked when you found out that the red color was not completely natural. Betrayed! Now, it elicits feelings of wariness – is it or isn't it?

Perhaps your family was very vocal and easily expressed emotions in both a verbal and physical way. Most of your siblings went along with the flow and behaved similarly. But you kept being embarrassed and wanting to hide away when such loud interactions occurred.

Addictions can come into play whether they were "out of control" or just something that came along for the ride. Smoking tobacco or marijuana, drinking alcohol, taking lots of legal drugs, or sneaking in amounts of illegal drugs; these become part of "normality" and will either attract or repulse you – and you may not know which (on the inside).

Your wish list will probably rule against anything currently considered undesirable – but today's fashions or standards will not substantially change your attraction list.

Perhaps your family gives lots of hugs. If these are sincere, unforced, hugs then you'll probably be comfortable with giving and receiving. But what if they were obligatory and not always comfortable? Were some behaviors acceptable from/by your brothers but not by you? (Or from/by your sisters.)

There are lots of behaviors that are part of your family dynamic. Some may be unique to your family. Some may not be considered "normal" or "healthy" but – to you – they are all part of what you experienced, They are all part of what you still expect even if you have decided that they weren't good.

Media and your Attraction List.

There's "no place like home" to build up a basic attraction list. But the less you interact with your family, the more influence outside aspects will have. Peer behaviors, and the families of peers, will substitute for your family

Media will also take its place. Movies, streaming video, podcasts, recordings, talk shows, TED talks, are part of what you absorb – the earlier in life it is, the more of a part of your "foundation" they will be.

What do they do? Currently, watching people smoke tobacco is considered to be something that is strongly discouraged. Thus, smoking may give a movie an automatic "R" rating. (Whether that discourages, or encourages, is another matter.) But there are other living behaviors that may, or may not, be part of ratings and exclusion/inclusion. Some of these are, once again, only able to be evaluated via your family history and context.

Fantasy and your Attraction List.

If there is something missing from your homelife – especially if you are aware (from others' situations) it is missing – you will likely fantasize about having it. Your mother is not around? Perhaps you will imagine Elizabeth

Montgomery (from "Bewitched") as your mother. Perhaps it will be a movie star such as Halle Berry.

Maybe you compare your father to a father in a television series and you think you would prefer your father to be more like the way you interpret the character. You may be looking at your father's actions with the other character a constant comparison.

Fantasy does not necessarily mean being an astronaut during a period when there is almost no space activity. It is using imagination to change what is, or add what is missing, to your daily life – and your attraction list.

Complementary Attractions.

Are you shy? You may be attracted to those who are outgoing and able to talk with anyone and about anything. Do you admire slender, athletic people but you, yourself, have difficulty getting out of your chair on a regular basis?

Sometimes a complementary attraction will work both directions. A shy person may be attracted to someone outgoing and the outgoing person is happy to have an audience with whom they will never be competing for attention.

Sometimes a complementary attraction does not work. If you admire slender, athletic people and you, yourself, cannot be described that way – how likely is it that that athletic person will be attracted to you? (But, remember that no attribute is in isolation – they may be attracted for other reasons and are willing to tolerate the reality that you will never go for long runs together.)

Either way, you will still have the attraction. Bring it to the surface, be aware of it, and you have the option of working to change yourself into someone who may be attractive to the person to whom you are attracted. Or recognize that that attribute is not a likely one to match.

Synergistic Attractions.

Synergistic attraction has a lot in common with complementary attraction. In both cases, you are aiming to make the relationship a more comprehensive package. For complementary, you are mainly looking for aspects that you feel that you miss. For synergistic, it may be qualities you lack or it may be properties you have. Instead of a more complete whole, you are aiming to make that "super-package" such that the sum is greater than the parts. You are both interested in politics – one person can be the front and the other can work with all the matters needed to keep campaigns going. Perhaps you are an author. You are great at plots and locations. They are great at dialog and consistency (plus a high attention to detail). A winning team.

You may be attracted to this situation. Since it should be a win/win, there is a possibility of it coming together. Being aware can help.

Your Attraction List is Not Going to Change – Accept It.

We have talked a lot about how an attraction list may be created. We have also talked about how it differs from a wish list. Bringing the attraction list out into the open can be very beneficial. You can recognize just what aspects attract you that cause the person to become your personal jerk.

Attraction lists are a set of attributes, much of which may be hidden in your subconscious. A wish list tells about things you believe would create a fulfilling, supportive, relationship. You may have a "healthy, calm, non-smoking, short, athletic person on your wish list and you may find yourself attracted to tall people who smoke and are not horribly out of shape but would never be considered athletic.

Even if you succeed in creating a fairly thorough attraction list, you may not understand WHY some aspects are on the list. For me, therapy was useful for doing such, You may find that useful, or you may be able to delve in with a friend to find those reasons. Once you know the attribute, and understand why, then you have the potential to say "I am attracted to this because of these reasons but I do not want it in my life. I choose to ignore my attraction."

If you are unaware, you WILL repeat. I have considerable doubts that, even with awareness, you can change your psyche to no longer be attracted.

If you are aware, you can make choices.

Chapter 4: Initiation & Maintenance

A significant problem, or set of problems, in our society is gender-role expectations. Within a potential heterosexual relationship, males are supposed to initiate – make the first move in asking out the other. And, after the second or third date, the female is expected to keep the relationship going. This relationship maintenance continues into marriage or other long-term commitment.

Societal Expectations.

Women relying on men to initiate the relationship cuts down the number of "healthy" males for them to potentially become involved with. It also increases the number of potentially abusive partners that will approach them. Yes, there will be men of a healthy character with self-confidence who want to become part of a healthy, nurturing, relationship. But, there will also will be plenty of males with a self-aggrandizing, forceful, aggressive personality who have no problems in pursuing a woman whether or not she has any interest. Such males do not CARE whether they are "harassing" or invading personal space or ignoring refusals. History tends to reinforce this approach as they have a much better chance of getting into a relationship with a woman than a caring, deferential, quiet male who cannot get himself to endure a potential rejection based on his societal requirement to initiate.

"Men can tell whether we want them to initiate." No, they can't. As a general rule, women are trained to be socially aware and supportive. Men aren't. Some males will be able to read body language and interpret "obvious" phrases like "I have to wash my hair tonight". But MOST will believe that you are telling the truth, be totally unable to read your body language, and continue to try (or just give up forever and you have thwarted another potential great relationship). The aggressive, high potential abusers, see no boundaries and will keep pressuring the women even if explicitly told to stop. The ones likely to abuse won't care about whether they are harassing and the ones likely to treat you like royalty may be too scared of being rejected, or considered to be harassing, to ever approach.

So, we have the perils of leaving initiation to the males – increasing the success rate of those who have higher potential to abuse and lowering the chances of getting involved with the "really good ones".

On the other hand, women shouldn't be the only ones who work on maintenance of a relationship. My father went through the various courtship activities and worked hard to do what my mother liked, as well as encourage her to become closer to him. But, he didn't consider that to be part of the ongoing relationship after marriage. My mother became more and more bitter and disillusioned and eventually went the divorce route which became very messy, my mother went on to husband number four, and my father did not survive.

Be Yourself or Be Sorry.

As some of the later suggestions indicate, you really need to "be yourself" during the initial phases of the relationship so that the same person will be manifest throughout your journey.

But that is only one aspect of maintenance. Just as women need to take on the responsibility of initiation to help steer society toward better health, men need to take on the tasks of maintenance. There are lots of articles on "sharing household responsibilities" – and, yes, that is one aspect of maintenance but other very important aspects are included in emotional maintenance. Men are not often trained in that so the journey may be difficult but the results can certainly be a healthier relationship as well as better modeling for future generations.

External versus Internal.

If your attraction list is specific about external characteristics then perhaps you may want to examine those aspects closely to see if you can succeed in overcoming them. Although wish lists often emphasize internal characteristics (less so for males), attraction lists can have a much greater emphasis on physical attributes than you may be aware of.

Perhaps they ARE that important to you; you are unable to maintain any closeness to people who do not meet your physical criteria. If you get involved with someone who does not meet your attraction criteria (and you are unaware that is going on) then you are more likely to "cheat" with someone else or not fully engage with your existing partner.

This is a huge reason to try to uncover, and be aware of, your attraction list. Not only can unawareness have you attracted to your next "jerk" but it can prevent you from fully committing to someone with whom you have a positive relationship but don't find sufficiently attractive.

Priorities.

At some point, people can decide that they are tired of hitting their head against a wall, just give up, and refuse to attempt to initiate. That can be quite understandable – no one wants to constantly court pain and rejection. And it may be the right thing to do at the time – once you have stopped looking for "M. right" then you may start relaxing with "platonic" relationships you have and find yourself deepening within them.

The topic of priorities can include the order of the items on your wish list or attraction list. But it also does include the general priorities of your life. You may tell a friend that "finding M. Right is the most important thing in my life" but making it top priority does not inherently increase your chances of success. Enjoy your life, expand your skills and interests, and allow other relationships to deepen and develop. You may be surprised that

1. You have more fun and enjoyment of life on an everyday basis and

2. You are more open to people in general and the possibility of one of them being "the one" increases.

Aggression versus Assertiveness.

There are two qualities that can seem very similar to someone looking from the "outside". They especially seem similar if you are in the "googly-eyed" stage. These qualities are aggression versus assertiveness.

These are very different because of change in focus. Someone who is aggressive will work strongly for themselves and their own needs and desires with little (or no) regard for others' needs. Someone who is assertive will defend their own needs and desires and will consistently keep them in mind when doing things and making commitments but they are not rigid. Compromise is possible with someone who is assertive and their assertive energy can extend to protecting the needs and desires of others (such as a partner).

Having read through the differences, it is easy to see how aggression may be mistaken for assertiveness; how a self-focused behavior can be mistaken for a position of strength in defending needs. If you can distinguish between the two early in the relationship, you may save pain (and possibly physical injury).

Anger versus Energy.

Anger is an indication, and release, of energy. When this energy is constructively channeled it can be used for useful, even miraculous, purposes. Unchanneled anger can be destructively expressed against you, themselves, groups, and so forth.

Most people can be aware of energy in a room and where is the focus of such energy. Different emotions can help to arouse energy but anger is one of the most manipulable. You can, with little energy or forethought, get someone angry. It is more difficult to make another joyous, or curious though these can also be a gateway.

Energy is attractive. Just like a moth dancing around a source of light, people will tend to gather around a focus of energy. Work to be sure it is an energy directed towards constructive matters.

Chapter 5: Self-Image & Self-Worth

"I don't deserve any better." "I must have done something wrong for her to hit me." "I must hang on to this man, even if he treats me like dirt, because I will never attract another." In our existing society, there are an awful lot of negative messages that we give ourselves and not nearly enough positive ones.

What is Loving Yourself?

This is NOT the same as "you can only love someone else if you love yourself". There are way too many narcissists out in the world who (at least on the surface) not only love themselves but feel that they are the only person in the world that matters. The type of love that this adage is concerned with is a much wider, and deeper, type of love that can be easily extended towards other people. It is an aspect of The Golden Rule. "Know thyself." Shoot, this is an area where adages exist by the dozens – and yet it is also an area in which we seem to have the greatest difficulties.

Loving yourself. Easy to say. Not easy for many of us to do. In my opinion, the core part of this capability is to accept yourself. That does not mean you don't have any desire to "improve" yourself (based on whatever criteria you use for such). But, as you are today, you have to accept yourself as you are. You're a klutz and can't move from room to room without tripping over the rugs at least once? Laugh and embrace your klutziness. It is a part of you and you will not become any more graceful (nor give yourself enticements to BECOME more graceful) if you spend your time dwelling on it. Your hair is turning grey? I got my first white hair at age 11. Although I recognize (more on this later) that the external appearance of women is often a much larger part of self-image than for men it is still something to embrace.

Societal Expectations.

In most of the consumeristic world, we are battered by advertisements that say we need to change, we need to buy something, there is no satisfaction in being who we are and with what we have. For women, those barrages are primarily sent against appearance – makeup, hairstyle & color, weight, clothing, artificial scent. For men it is less focused on appearance (though it still happens) but you need to have that great car, great phone, style of pants or so forth. Dress for success.

It seems to be true that males, in general, are attracted primarily by visual cues. But just WHAT those cues are can be manipulated by society – local and more general. Religious people can either be attracted to, or repulsed by, accepted symbols displayed by others. This is not innate but part of growing up in that religion and the experiences thereof. I, myself, grew up in "blue-collar" neighborhoods and "dressing for success" is not something with which I am comfortable nor appreciate as a positive thing.

People who are well aware of their own feelings and that of others may choose to put on a façade to "blend in" to the societal expectations of the group in which they want to be included. "Fake it until you make it" CAN work but recognize that you would need to be choosing changes within yourself based on expectations. You can change only if you, yourself, want to do so.

Self-confidence Hidden by Shyness.

You don't need to be in the middle of things or the life of the party to have self-confidence. It is totally possible to still be shy and retiring away from others and still be self-confident. It isn't a question of how much of yourself you "can put out there". It is a question of how much of yourself you can retain.

Be a self-confident introvert. You still have need of assertiveness or you can find that others are trying to take from you for their own desires. Some are able to be more themselves in writing or online. Others are okay with being verbal and present if it is a one-on-one situation.

You can be shy and assertive. You can be shy and have self-confidence. You can be shy and feel self-worth. Shyness is independent of these qualities and you don't need to be defensive about such. You DO need to stand up for yourself via assertiveness and the ability to accept who you are.

Localized Behaviors (body comfort, caring, etc.).

Rubenesque. That is (especially for women) bodily sculpted like the well-rounded, curvaceous, people that Rubens painted. Throughout much of history, the ideal female shape has been larger and curvier – more able to withstand periodic lack of food, to be able to continue to sustain a pregnancy without danger to herself or the child. This is a biologic attraction. Twiggy triggered a modern thin ideal for women. There are also studies, and theories, about the best body weight or best fat/non-fat ratio for people. Maybe so. But being happy about the way you are is much more likely to give you both health and a smile.

For men, there is a desire to be "strong" and "supportive". The societal ideal for such has not been constant over the years. For a lot of societies, gender roles have been quite distinct – especially for those who could afford to be picky (the wealthier, "upper", strata of society). Everyone needed to pitch in if the family was just trying to survive. "Gentlemanly" and "lady-like" behaviors declines in importance in comparison to being able to live.

Different societal strata have different standards and expectations. Some cultures even have different languages based on gender and social level. Some will idealize people with darkened skin (solar encouraged pigmentation) and others will idealize those with non-darkened skin. It changes. When tanned skin was an indication of working outside as labor, it was not considered attractive. But, when tanned skin indicated the ability to have leisure to pamper oneself, it became an area of "beauty".

Eye color, height, "love handles", ... They exist and the perception thereof is truly in the eye, and society, of the beholder.

You are you. You are fantastic the way you are. Those others who do not treat you that way are probably deserving to be placed in the "jerk" category. Keep going and find the one who appreciates you.

Where Did that Come From?

You may find yourself attracted to – and consider yourself worthy of attraction – based on non-obvious criteria. Big feet, little feet, wavy hair, straight hair, six fingers per hand or five fingers per hand, all attributes that may make you feel more worthy or less worthy.

The chances are good that they are based on what you are used to seeing and the emotional connection you have with those characteristics. They will be part of your attraction list and they will also be part of your self-image evaluation.

We come back to the beginning of the chapter. Accept yourself. Find others that will also accept you. Wherever it comes from, no matter how many, or few, people consider it good or bad – roll with it and be the person you are.

Chapter 6: Pedestals, Perfection, & Tolerance

Especially in the "googly-eyed" stage – but potentially in every stage, if you are attracted to someone then you will want to justify that attraction. They don't have this attribute from my wish list but they do have this one. Maybe the missing attribute isn't that important and the attribute they DO have is more important than I thought.

Deliberately ignoring things that you said you didn't want is a problem. But trying to just sweep it off your desk and say "this person is perfect, my ideal, my hope diamond. They belong in an art museum perched on a marble pedestal."). Search for that flaw in the diamond as quickly as possible.

You are very unlikely to find someone who has all of your wish list credentials AND all of your attraction list specifics AND those other attributes you failed to note down. There will be negative (from your perspective) things that you must tolerate. Be aware of what you are tolerating. Make it a choice.

Pedestals are Designed to be Fallen Off of.

Pedestals are designed for busts, maybe small statues, or perhaps a potted plant. They aren't designed for people (or elephants, or even squirrels). The idea of a pedestal is to bring something up, off the floor, to have better access to it and a better view of it. With that elevation comes risk. A statue on the floor might be toppled but it won't fall. A bird cage on the floor tipped over doesn't greatly change its functionality. A bird cage fallen from a pedestal may no longer have the integrity needed to house the bird.

Sometimes people think that (usually figuratively but occasionally literally) putting people on a pedestal is a good thing. Maybe, but not often. It is hard for the person looking towards the pedestal, putting them on a different, lower, level than the one on the pedestal. The person on the pedestal must spend much of their energy trying not to fall off the pedestal. It is a lose/lose situation.

I can imagine exceptions but that exception (never falling off the pedestal) seems like a much greater fantasy than whatever provoked the person to put you there.

It is possible to admire characteristics and still be aware of the whole person – "warts" and all. This doesn't necessarily have to occur in the "googly-eyed" stage but it should be treated as the same. Get over it as soon as possible.

If Perfection is Your Goal, Prepare for Disappointment.

Perfection. The first definition of the word "perfect" is "complete". So, a person who is completely clumsy may have their walking described as perfect – but almost no one will use the word in that manner. For most people, they treat the word the same as they do "luck". If I wish you luck, I MIGHT mean "bad luck" but the assumption is that I wish you good luck. Thus, for almost all people, the word perfection means completely good, completely positive, complete in all positive attributes.

And it just isn't possible except in religious figures as seen from later years. That perfect person will eventually demonstrate that they do not meet the lofty standards upon which you have given them. No one can. Many (most) will attribute this to the other during the "googly-eyed" stage while critical facilities are greatly reduced or banished. But, that stage does pass.

Don't expect perfection.

Moderate the Attraction Points You do Not Want.

If no one is perfect (expanding to completely positive), then they have positive points and negative points. Once again, as per the beginning of the book, this is from YOUR perspective. They are aspects that may make them a "jerk" (negative points) or make them "M. Right" (positive points).

Pitting the wish list against the attraction list, you theoretically want all of those things on the wish list. But your attraction list only moderately compares to your wish list.

To improve the chances that this person will be someone that you truly want to remain with, shove back those attraction aspects you don't want (be aware but reluctant to accept).

Self-control with Awareness.

It would be great if I could just tell you "squelch everything on your attraction list that doesn't match your wish list" and go for your wish list. The problem is that your attractions are not going away. Have you ever told yourself "I know I don't like that but ..."? You are going to have to tolerate some things that you believe that you don't like. It is quite possible that you have ordered your wish list – maybe categorized them. "Must have", "Really hope to have" and "Nice to have".

Categorizing your attraction list is much more complex. You have things like "have got to have", "must not have", "really would like to have", "greatly prefer not to have", and "who cares". As mentioned in the chapter on Awareness Lists, the positive things on your attraction list aren't so important to isolate and acknowledge. If you aren't aware that you are attracted to red hair then is that important? But, if you are attracted to people who will physically abuse you, you MUST be aware of such.

The only real value to knowing about "positive" things on your attraction list is to understand yourself better. That's a good thing but the positives aren't going to matter in your journey to avoid the "jerks" in your life.

If you are aware, you can choose to suppress or enhance. It won't necessarily be easy but if you are not aware you won't know what is happening.

Attraction Can Grow with Support.

If there is something in the person, with whom you are trying to deepen into a relationship, that you just don't find attractive (hopefully not quite to the point of repulsiveness), there is hope. Although you are not likely ever to eliminate anything from your attraction list, you are still growing, still learning, and still adapting. If your attraction list had no hope of expanding then there isn't much point in continuing to have experiences. How could a 70-year-old in 1970 ever find that they loved to watch Jeopardy!, and was attracted to other people with that love, if the list could not grow? The first television broadcast wasn't until 1925 and the first episode of Jeopardy! didn't happen until 1964.

You have to be willing to try, and keep trying. Maybe you have never really enjoyed food and cooking because your father was a terrible cook and you still remember when he burned your cake for your seventh birthday. But your potential partner loves to cook and feels buoyed by appreciation for the food they prepare. Isn't that worth trying to learn something new?

Chapter 7: Cultural Incompatibilities

"Vive la difference!" Yes, this French phrase is usually applied to the appreciation of sexual differences in a relationship between a man and a woman. But, it is true that differences can add to a relationship. They can give more areas to learn, and appreciate, about your partner. Given a desire to appreciate, the fact that you are both different, with different interests and strengths, gives the potential to have a stronger, and more capable, situation as a couple.

Foundational Behaviors.

The very fact that you are different is not inherently a problem and may be a blessing. It depends on attitude. If you go into a relationship expecting, even demanding, changes in behaviors of the other person then it does not bode well for the ongoing health of either. Whereas tolerance, and even potential appreciation, of those differences will add to the relationship. Tolerance can even lead to self-imposed changes by the other person as they see how much something means to you and how much you care about them even though they continue to do it.

But incompatibilities, or tolerated differences, rarely lead to situations where jerkdom starts being invoked. It is much more likely when there are implicit behaviors which are unknown to the other originally and which are a core aspect of the history, and behavior, of the person

One such implicit set of behaviors is involved with cultural expectations. For much of human history, societies have been patriarchal with limited, and specific, behaviors expected from women. For a large part of the world, this situation is shifting towards a more cooperative partnership with both people being part of both the decision making and the (paid and unpaid) work.

People who accept the more recent relationship behaviors will often object to the older relationships. And those who continue to be a willing part of the older style relationships may be uncomfortable with, and object to, the more recent variety of relationships. Note the word "willing" as it does acknowledge that changes in society happen as those unwilling to continue the status quo make steps to move away from the old and towards the new. This change can be very hard, especially without a strong support group, and even dangerous.

Being a bit less wordy, let's summarize. If one person raised in a role-assigned environment becomes involved with someone who expects equalitarian treatment then conflict is quite possible. Toleration and appreciation are needed to smooth the waves.

Once Again – Be Yourself.

As many suggestions have indicated, you really need to "be yourself" during the relationship. When dating, consciously or not, each tries to impress and present a person that will be appreciated by the other. Being other than "ourselves" is not something which helps the later relationship but, nonetheless, it does happen. Also, until a couple is functioning as a couple there are many things about life that are not known or explicitly discussed.

But once the relationship is more formalized, true behaviors will take hold and expectations will arise. And, thus, jerkdom starts raising its head. The person being a "jerk" will not agree that they are not behaving well – they may even strongly believe that the poor behavior is coming from the other person. Both are right – they have fallen into an incompatible cultural relationship.

A expects both to share in decision making. B expects to be solely in charge of all decisions. A expects chores to be allocated according to time available and less pleasant chores are distributed across the relationship. B thinks that there are certain duties that are appropriate for each of them and they should each do such and be happy within their roles.

If A and B have the same expectations and are within a voluntary, willing, relationship then there is no problem. But, as society changes, there is greater likelihood of people not being in sync with expectations of the other.

Note that, if B grew up in a matriarchal family (as did I), many of the behaviors of the stereotypical genders get reversed.

Chapter 8: Blame

Neither blaming another person for being a jerk nor blaming yourself for getting involved with a jerk is productive. The other person is who they are – some may consider them a jerk but others will probably not consider them a jerk. These chapters are aimed at getting you to examine yourself and your interactions with others such that you will no longer get involved (or, at least, not for long) with those YOU consider to be a jerk. It is our hope that, as you increase knowledge of yourself, you can both allow better relationships to begin and be able to better sustain healthy relationships.

Blame is never useful. The goal is to improve. Isolation of reasons, and people, involved in a negative situation may tempt a person into blaming but blaming is both a lack of acceptance of people as they are and a defeatist attitude that indicates no improvement is possible.

Blame is a Combination of Guilt and Fear.

What is this feeling we call blame? It is not a basic emotion. It is a combination of guilt (telling yourself it is your fault at some level) and fear (of repeating the situation or that consequences of the situation may not be surmountable). When we hear about a recall of a product, or a problem in a product that has caused damage or harm, we naturally wonder how it happened. We wonder who was involved. Can we trust the person, or company, that is responsible for the problem in the future?

Internally, companies who are involved with such situations will attempt to determine what happened and who was involved. Good (well run) companies will use this information to improve. Bad (poorly run) companies will find people to blame, get rid of them, and pretend that that will prevent any future problems. Sometimes they will not be able to isolate problems to any known individuals. In such conditions, a poorly run company will choose an individual to blame – to be a scapegoat.

The same dynamics can occur within personal relationships. We want to understand, improve, and continue with our lives. Blaming yourself or the other casts an illusion that all problems revolved around that person. And it will not improve.

Use the Past.

Don't beat yourself up about what you did, or what happened, in the past. You can't change it – but you CAN learn from it. If certain people were unreliable – stop relying on them unless you feel almost certain that they have truly changed. Be aware of yourself as much as you can (I believe that it can be done without therapy – just use a "good mate" to bounce things off of as Crocodile Dundee once said) and then use that awareness to re-evaluate the events of the past.

What would you do differently if the same set of circumstances happened again? More importantly, what would you LIKE to do differently if the same set of circumstances happened again? These two questions are not the same. You may need to work on something, or gain new skills, or change your side of the interactions in some way so that you CAN do it differently.

Decide for the Present.

Lots of philosophical quotes are concerned about the past, present, and future. A lot of them are probably true.

It is a matter of perspective and in what way you learn. As mentioned in the previous paragraph, the past is present as a reservoir of experience (and it doesn't have to be YOUR experience). That experience is USED for the present.

The present is the only thing you have control over. Make decisions. React constructively to what is happening. Prepare for the future but don't make precise roadmaps for the future. You want to be prepared for many different paths even if your current goal is directed one direction.

Learn for the Future.

Since you have reached the eighth chapter of this book, I'll assume that one of your goals is to be in a relationship with a non-jerk. Hopefully, this book will be useful. However, this book is only a set of things to look at, a few tools to use, and perhaps a change of perspective allowing you a fresh look at yourself. You still need to work at moving forward.

Learn for the Future, Use the Past.

Sometimes, repetition is just part of the game. Just as you may have been in multiple relationships, repetition of advice from slightly different wordings and perspectives may make better sense.

You have a past. It may have a lot of events or experiences that you didn't enjoy (hopefully, it also has such that you DID enjoy). If you can examine those experiences then you can learn, you can change reactions and decisions, and you can succeed.

Chapter 9: Commitment

Chapter before the summary. Congratulations! This chapter diverges from the whole idea of "jerks" and how to choose your next non-jerk.

You have found your "non-jerk"! The relationship is getting closer, sharing is happening, and you are turning the situation into a desired relationship. Now you have to keep it (or, at least, keep it as long as it nurtures).

Every long-term relationship has problems. Things happen. Tragedies happen. Opportunities happen (sometimes the successes put more stress on a relationship than the failures). I say that it has problems but maybe it doesn't. But if it doesn't experience changes then you are both locked into a set of tanks dreaming in the Matrix.

Changes mean continuous adaptation – for ALL involved in the relationship. If one person seems to be doing all of the adjusting, take a closer look. Why is this happening? Is it healthy for everyone in the relationship?

There are different levels of commitment, of course. There is the commitment to be "steady" (which usually means exclusive – though any consensual agreement can work). There is a commitment of a promise to the future ("engaged" – which should not only be "steady" but should be preparing for being in a publicly committed partnership). Finally, there is a public commitment in front of family, friends, and possibly a religious authority. Some type of public commitment should be part of a marriage.

This final level of public commitment means you are all committed to make it work. There should not be an easy out at this point. You should have explored sufficiently before public commitment such that – as you both are at that point in time – you are comfortable in making a serious (expected to last forever) commitment.

Life is change. People can change. You made a serious public commitment, in the circumstances that existed at that point, to the other. But no one should be required to suffer until death. They are in an accident, hurt badly, become addicted to drugs, start being hateful and abusive – you don't deserve that. They go into therapy and discover within themselves unexpected aspects (perhaps a presumed heterosexual finds they have been suppressing homosexual genetic urges due to societal pressures). No one deserves to be suffering ever after.

But no easy out. Try, try, try.

The following sections should be BEFORE you make that final public commitment.

Is What Exists Sufficient?

Is it enough? You have a wish list. You have an attraction list. You have an awareness of what is on the attraction list and have moderated it to allow only those items you are willing (or want) to live with. Is it enough? If you are continuously looking around and evaluating others WHILE YOU ARE IN THE RELATIONSHIP then you have a problem and the relationship has a problem. Even in the "steady" step of commitment, you should be concentrating on the person with whom you are hoping will be the one.

If you are still looking around then back off. Give both of you the freedom to look around. Maybe you'll come back when you are both ready. Maybe you need to find someone else.

Can You Tolerate Imperfection?

Although you do want the match to be good "enough", it is very unlikely (personally, I would say impossible) that everything will match, there are no frictions or difficulties, and you will be 100% happily ever after.

Can you tolerate those imperfections? You must assume that they will NOT change. You can point them out (constant pointing out goes by another name – nagging) so they will know that you would like them to know that you want them to want to change (phew, try saying that quickly). But you have to assume NO. Can you accept them as they are? If not, do not continue. Back off, be friends and keep looking.

What Happens When you Hit the Hard Spots?

Do you have a plan about what to do when you hit the hard spots? Have you already allocated the couch (or dog house) for one of you? Temporary distance may help.

You need to look things over again. Depending on how far you have gone along the commitment path, you may need to evaluate if this will work. It is completely possible that you may find someone who is not a "jerk" according to your standards – but they are still not a "M. Right".

And that's okay at the early stages of commitment. If you are farther along when you realize the situation, then you need to not only look back but also re-evaluate to not have it happen again.

Looking Back and Looking Forward.

Same section title. Slightly different subject manner. As you prepare to commit, you need to examine what has been done in the past. Apparently, you felt you had been involved with a "jerk" in the past (otherwise, why are you reading this?). You may have also been in a committed relationship that was heading for the next step.

What happened within that relationship? What went wrong? What went right? Did you learn anything from it? Do you feel comfortable at ending a commitment at the beginning and also comfortable with sticking it out within a publicly committed relationship at the end?

Are you Ready for Success?

People often think of "what if I fail?". Sometimes, people have more difficulty with, and have thought much less about, having success with their search. Are you ready for success? What does that mean? How will they support you and how will you support them? Is there a synergy you were hoping for? Children? Retirement home?

The future is what you make of it.

In It for the Long Haul.

"A Long and Winding Road, that Leads ..., to your Door". Life is strange. Life is a series of changes, actions, reactions, and continuations. And it's YOUR life.

Keep on trucking.

Chapter 10: Summary – How NOT to be Involved with a Jerk

BE YOURSELF! The point of dating is to determine how you work together and how well you can live together (it is not mandatory to physically live together first). If you are presenting someone other than yourself – then you are going to have problems, perhaps, fatal ones, in the relationship as you each discover who "the real you" is. If you are jogging every day with your potential mate and you hate jogging – well, that WILL be a problem. If you love watching certain anime and it is important to you to be able to share it with a partner and your partner dutifully watches it with you but hates every minute – that WILL be a problem.

COMMUNICATE! This is needed within all relationships. Practice active listening where, by use of questions, you clarify that you have heard what the other person meant to say. Don't suppress important (preferably don't suppress any) information because it "isn't important" or "won't matter" or for purposes of control.

This includes secrets – if it is something that will matter when/if it is ever discovered, think really carefully about hiding it as you are burying a live bomb.

LEARN HOW TO MAKE DECISIONS! Maybe one person does all the decision-making. Maybe you make decisions together (taking into account "being yourself" and "communicating"). Maybe you use a Tarot deck or a dart board. Anything is possible but you must know how you are going to do it and be happy with the process. Decisions are a vital part of growth, and ability to adapt to change, within a relationship.

SELF-EXAMINE and IMPROVE! Okay, you made a poor decision and got involved with a jerk. Why? What can you do differently to make it different next time. Don't spend any time ranting and raving about what the other person did. (You're certainly allowed some anger and sadness – this is a failed investment of time and hope.) Concentrate on the one person you have influence on – YOU.

Let's raise a glass to toast the healthy relationship to come that you deserve!

List of Publications

Technical
ISDN Implementor's Guide, Mc-Graw Hill, 1995.
ISDN: How to Get a High-Speed Connection to the
      Internet (w/Bryant Dunetz), John Wiley & Sons, 1996.
ADSL: Standards, Implementation, and
      Architecture, CRC Press, 1999.

Non-Fiction
The First 100: Ideas and Interpretations,
      Charles K. Summers, 2020.
The Second 100: Ideas and Interpretations,
      Charles K Summers, 2022.
The Third 100: Ideas and Interpretations, Charles K
      Summers, 2025.
Why Am I Involved with a Jerk ... AGAIN?,
      Charles K. Summers, 2025.

Middle-grade and Young Adult Fiction
The Taylor Twins and the Ghost Club,
      Charles K Summers, 2013.
The Taylor Twins and the Pirate Cave,
      Charles K Summers, 2023.
Rumblings in the Reef, Charles K Summers, 2025.

https://charlesksummers.com
https://charlesksummers.substack.com

NOTES

NOTES

NOTES

NOTES

NOTES

NOTES

NOTES

NOTES

NOTES

NOTES

NOTES

NOTES

NOTES

NOTES

NOTES

NOTES

NOTES

NOTES

NOTES

NOTES

NOTES

NOTES

NOTES

www.ingramcontent.com/pod-product-compliance
Lightning Source LLC
LaVergne TN
LVHW022012080426
835513LV00009B/685